Tall Tales from a Tiny Town

A Collection of Funny Stories

Warren Robinson

LENOX
DINR

TABLE OF CONTENTS

Introduction

I was born in 1945, just as World War II was about to close. Those were magical times in the little town of Lenox, Georgia during the late 1940s and 1950s.

I was the youngest of the three children of Blanche and Roby Robinson. My mother came to Lenox as a first-grade school teacher where she met and married my father. My dad was President, Chairman and CEO of Bank of Lenox. The bank was founded by his dad in 1906s.

I remember walking the half mile to school every day, sometimes in freezing weather and sometimes it was blistering heat, but I never paid the weather much attention. Every day was a new adventure. After school, I put on my back pack with my lunch bucket and walked the same path back home. On most days, I stopped off at my dad's bank where he would let me play on the manual adding machine. Most days, he would give me a nickel or a dime which I would promptly spend buying a bag of candy from Mr. Godwin's General Merchandise store next door.

Most of all, I remember the people of our small town. Everybody knew everybody else and it was just one big, extended family. Speaking of which is the focus of this book. The following chapters will illuminate some of the unique characters of Lenox. I hope these stories will put a smile on your face and make your day a little brighter.

I have traveled most of the world and there are certainly many beautiful places I enjoy seeing, but I am always glad to see my little hometown. My family and I have been blessed beyond anything we could ever deserve, and I rejoice at any chance to give back to it.

Judge H. W. Lott

The Early Years

The memory of Judge H. W. Lott and his wife, Stella, will always stand out in my memory. They were both outstanding citizens and beloved by everyone who knew them. This first chapter is devoted to them because of the special status they held in my family's life. I can just imagine Judge and Stella reading these words and having a good laugh.

My first recollection of Judge Lott occurred long before he became a Superior Court Judge in the Alapaha Judicial Circuit. On afternoon, my dad and I were sitting on the front of the screened porch facing the dirt road. I remember a black sedan speeding down the road and raising a huge cloud of dust as it seemed to turn the corner at our house on two wheels, headed for the turpentine still just down the road. My dad made an offhand remark, “Well, there goes H. W. with another load of shine.” I didn’t understand what “shine” meant, but by the way my dad said the word, I knew it was not good.

Up until the early 1950s, Lenox had no paved streets, no city water, no city sewer system and we heated our home with coal burning in the fireplace.

That was about the time we had an old black, hand cranked telephone. We drew water from our own well, we used an outhouse and we gathered eggs from our chicken house in the back yard. Sometimes I remember my mother and her maid, Sylvia, catching chickens and wringing their necks until they were dead. Then the nasty part began, cleaning them.

During the summer, dad always had a large garden on the lot next door and we all gathered fresh vegetables that were later taken to the canning plant in Adel. Mother always canned enough vegetables to take us through to the next summer. Every Saturday, my dad would hand mother a $20.00 dollar bill, which she took downtown and purchased enough groceries to feed all five of us for the entire week.

I remember my dad was elected Mayor of Lenox and sometimes I would accompany him the city council meetings. Citizens began to ask why our town didn't have running water, like some of the larger towns nearby. The answer was always that the little town didn't have the money to install a central water system. Nobody wanted to raise property taxes and there seemed to be no way to afford such a costly project. In those days, there were no state or federal grants for such things. Finally, someone proposed the idea of allowing liquor, beer and wine to be sold in town and the tax on it would be used to pay for a water system.

Naturally, there was a bitter battle between the dry votes and the wet votes. The wet votes eventually won in a referendum taken to decide the issue and all forms of alcohol were made legal for sale and a city tax was levied on it to pay for the water system which was installed sometime in 1949.

Saturday afternoons, dad would give us kids our weekly allowance, 25 cents each. With that quarter, the three of us, most times accompanied by my first cousin, Frederick Robinson, and our friend Sandra Godwin, would set out for the movie theatre owned and operated by Mr. Nelse Bennett and his wife. The ticket price was ten cents, a cold coke was five cents and a large bag of fresh popcorn was 10 cents. The theatre kept us entertained for most of the afternoon.

Before we left home for the theatre, mother would caution us not to walk down the street where a new honky tonk had been established by a young H. W. Lott. I remember one occasion when our curiosity got the better of us and we all approached the bar window. Inside, I remember seeing H. W. pouring a draft beer with his left hand and turning the page of a law book he was studying.

H. W. had graduated from high school and entered Mercer University as a law student. In those days, a college degree was not required.

The bar he ran on weekends provided the financing for H. W. to obtain his law school education.

Judge Lott and the Reckless Driver

One day, Judge Lott was on his way to hold court in the county seat of Adel when a young driver sped past the judge and almost forced him into the ditch. The incident infuriated him, and he sped up to stay right behind the reckless driver. The traffic light in Sparks turned red just in time to stop the young driver. Judge Lott immediately left his car and ran up to the offender, shouting, “Stop your car, you’re under citizen’s arrest.”

The Sparks Police was parked nearby and immediately came forward to the scene where Judge Lott explained what had just happened. The Judge proceeded to the courthouse as the Police officer took the young man into custody. The Officer immediately drove the young man to the courthouse and led him up the back stairs that led to the courtroom. On their way up, the young man asked the Officer, "Who was that little SOB shouting, you're under citizen's arrest?"

The officer informed him he was about to find out. The officer opened the courtroom door and pointed the boy to the bench where Judge Lott sat fully robed. It was reported that the young man turned pale and almost fainted.

Judge Lott and the Two Sisters

At times, Judge Lott made rulings that would make Solomon smile. A case in point was when two sisters who lived in the Lenox area inherited a farm jointly. As the years passed, one sister moved far away and wanted to sell her half interest in the farm, while the other had a strong sentimental attachment to it and wanted to keep her half. They could never agree upon a price, nor could they agree on how to physically divide the property itself. The bickering continued for many years and eventually ended up in court as the last resort to solve the problem. Judge Lott patiently heard testimony from both sides. Then, almost straight out of the Bible, he had the clerk fetch a large map of the property and mount it on an easel so it was visible to everyone in the courtroom. Then he handed a pen to one of the sisters and instructed her to go to the map and draw a dividing line that she considered to be a fair division of the property. The lady did as instructed and sat down. Then the judge told the other sister she had the first pick of which half she wanted. The case was finally settled, and one sister sold her half while the other one kept hers.

Judge Lott and the Blueberry Muffins

Judge Lott loved blueberry muffins and Stella would always have a batch freshly baked and ready for him when came home. He finally retired but continued trying cases as a senior judge in other circuits. One day he received a request to try a murder case in Albany, Georgia. It seems a prominent physician died under mysterious circumstances and the prosecutor had charged the physician's wife with murder in the first degree. The case was very sensational and it was revealed that the physician was killed by the consumption of cyanide. The prosecution was finally able to prove the wife had been adding small amounts of the poison to her husband's favorite treat each day. Yep, you guessed it!

Blueberry muffins!

That afternoon Stella greeted H. W. with a warm and freshly made batch of muffins as usual. H. W. told her politely he had lost his taste for the muffins and never ate another.

Judge Lott and the Eye Witness

An African American man had been shot and killed on the front porch of his home late one night. The only light was from a dim 60-watt bulb in an overhead socket. There was one man who claimed to be an eye witness to the crime. The defense attorney put him on the witness stand and questioned him. The man was steadfast in his testimony about seeing the murder happen and he positively identified the defendant as the perpetrator.

When the defense finished with the witness, the prosecutor had his cross-examination of the witness. The attorney was convinced it would be no problem to get the witness to admit there was no way he could make such a positive identification. He was able to get the man to admit he was 80 years-old, the event took place three blocks away from his home on a dark night when there was no moon. The only light was a dim little 60-watt bulb, and finally, the witness admitted his vision had faded considerably.

Feeling very confident now, the attorney questioned the man, “Are you asking this court to believe an 80-year-old man with diminishing vision, on a dark night could positively identify another man as the killer some three blocks away? “Just how far can you see on a dark night?”

The courtroom was deathly silent as everyone waited for the man to give his answer. He took his time considering the question, and finally answered in a very confident voice, “Why I can see all the way to the moon!”

With that, the courtroom erupted in laughter as the Judge banged for order in the court. Later, other evidence was presented that helped prove the old man was correct.

Judge Lott Holds Court in Berrien County

A brother and sister were having a bitter dispute about the validity of their father's will. One claimed he had bequeathed everything to him and the other claimed he had bequeathed everything to her. One day the sister was called to testify and as she left the witness chair, she passed close by her brother. She said to her brother in a somewhat loud voice, "You'll never get away with this you little SOB." The brother's attorney leaped to his feet and inquired, "Judge, did you hear what the last witness said to my client when she just walked by?

The Judge replied, "Yes, I heard her." The attorney was so angry his face was red with rage as he asked, "Well, aren't you going to challenge her about that slanderous remark?" The Judge replied cooly, "Well I started to, but I decided not to because I was afraid she might be able to prove it."

Judge Lott and the Dove Hunt

The next story is about a dove hunt Judge Lott hosted on his farm. I was invited, but could not attend for some reason. I have always regretted not being able to see this happen in person.

A young DNR Officer was on one of his first patrols in West Berrien County when he drove by Judge Lott's farm. Suddenly, he heard gunfire coming from somewhere not visible from the road. He decided to investigate and pulled off the main road onto the farm path that led in the direction he had heard the gunfire.

As he got closer, he could see a cornfield and at least a dozen pickup trucks parked adjacent to the woods. As he exited his truck, a middle-aged man walked by carrying a bag full of birds, obviously more than the daily limit. He topped the gentleman and asked to see his hunting license. The man looked annoyed, but did as he was asked. The license had expired and when he examined the man's gun, it too was in violation because it held five shells instead of three as called for in the regulations.

The young man retrieved his ticket book and proceeded to fill out a violation ticket. The hunter made no argument. A gentleman nearby felt compelled to inform the young man what was going on, so he pulled him aside and asked him if he knew who the man was he had just written the ticket for. The young officer replied that he had no idea who the hunter was since he had just moved into the area for his new job. The bystander informed him that the hunter was a Superior Court Judge in a nearby judicial Circuit. The bystander then took the young officer around and introduced him to all the other hunters. One was a State Senator from that district, another was the District Attorney, the head of the

Georgia State Patrol, several County Sheriffs and City Police Chiefs.

After meeting everyone, the young officer started making his way back to his truck as he cautioned them to be careful and have a good hunt all while he was ripping up the ticket he had just written for the judge.

Judge Lott and the IRS

One time before he met Stella, the Judge received one of those letters we all hate to find in our mailbox. It was a letter from the IRS informing him his tax return for the previous year had been selected for audit. The letter set out a date and time he was to meet with the agent in her office in Albany. He was instructed to bring all the supporting documents he had used to complete his return. Naturally, the Judge was nervous about the outcome of the audit and feared he would owe considerable extra taxes.

On the scheduled date, he entered the agent's office and had a seat. He had expected to see an unattractive, older woman. Much to his surprise, that was not what he saw seated at the desk opposite him. The agent was young and most attractive.

The audit began and lasted most of the day. Finally, the agent said they should call it quits and continue with the audit the following day. That's when the Judge stated he had not eaten all day and was very hungry. He also asked if the pretty agent would like to accompany him. She immediately that it would not be possible as long as they had not completed his audit. A few days later, the audit was completed and much to his surprise, the Judge was notified he would receive a $200.00 refund.

Judge Lott and the Egotistical Attorney

A case was scheduled to be tried in Adel on a certain day and it appeared there would be a bitter battle between the two parties. When the appointed date and hour arrived, the plaintiff was present with his client; however, the defendant and his attorney failed to appear. A jury had already been selected and everyone was wondering what would happen. The Judge decided to give the defense an extra 15 minutes to appear, but they never showed up. He picked up his gavel and was about to announce that the plaintiff had won the case by default.

Suddenly, the plaintiff's attorney asked if he could approach the bench and speak with the Judge. He was told to come forward, and the Judge was totally surprised when the attorney told him he had been a long-time admirer of the Judge and had always wanted to try a case before him. He stated that since a jury had already been impaneled and he had spent countless hours preparing his arguments; he asked to be allowed to go forward and make his statements to the jury. The Judge was very reluctant and warned the attorney that he had already achieved a win for his client since the defense failed to appear. The attorney pleaded to let the trial go forward and get a jury verdict for his client.

The Judge reluctantly agreed and the trial proceeded. The jury obviously had become aggravated since there was no point in detaining them for a one-sided argument.

After the plaintiff's attorney completed his arguments, the jury was dismissed to deliberate and reach a unanimous verdict. The attorney was very proud of himself, thinking he had made a convincing argument. The jury was led back into the jury box and the Judge asked if they had reached a unanimous verdict. The jury foreman rose and answered they had. Then the bailiff was called to fetch the verdict from the foreman and deliver it to the Judge. The egotistical attorney had his balloon deflated as the Judge announced the jury had found the case in favor of the defendant who had failed to appear.

Some Robinson Tales

J. D. Robinson

The Principal

My grandfather, J. D. Robinson, applied for the job as Elementary School principal at the small town of Eldorado. J.D. was a young man seeking an easier way to earn a living besides farming. He heard the previous Principal at Eldorado was forced to quit because he could not control the rowdy student body. J. D. knew he could control a bunch of kids.

No one else applied for the job after word spread that the old principal had been run out of town on a rail, so to speak, so the job was all his.

When the first day of school convened, J. D. convened the student body in the school auditorium. He decided to start this new school year on the right foot. He told the students the days tolerating their misbehavior were over.

To make his warnings believable, he ordered all the students to line up outside. He followed them after he grabbed his sturdy paddle with the hole in the middle. He told the students if they misbehaved in any way, what they were about to experience would only be a taste of what they would receive later. Then, he proceeded down the line and gave each student a sound spanking with the paddle. Then he dismissed them and sent them home.

The next day, the father of one of the boys who had received a spanking the day before came stomping into his office. The man said he wanted to know if J. D. had spanked his son for no reason whatever. J. D. stood up and replied yes, I did, and if you'll step outside, I'll whup your ass too!" The school had no more disciplinary problems from that day on.

J. D. Robinson, The Banker

My grandfather, J.D. Robinson, quit his teaching career after only one year. Shortly thereafter, he moved to Lenox where he became a very successful entrepreneur. He established a hardware store, was in a joint venture in a mule barn business, sold insurance for Woodmen of the World, established Cook County's first dairy farm, was a real estate broker, owned several large farms and last, but not least, helped establish The Bank of Lenox.

During J.D.s banking career, he helped many people purchase farms and he provided financing to plant and grow crops.

One of his close friends died, and in a few weeks, his widow, Sally came to the bank to chat with J.D. He asked her what she had decided to do about the farm. Sally said she had decided to keep the farm and continue growing crops. She said she had worked alongside her late husband for many years, and she felt confident she could carry on.

Sally then told J.D. she needed to borrow $200.00 to pay for seed and fertilizer for the next crop. J. D. responded that he would be delighted to make her the loan, but first, he would need a little "collateral". Sally had never borrowed money before and was very puzzled about what the word meant. Then her face lit up with a big smile and she replied, "Why J.D., you know I ain't done that kind of thing in years!" J.D. decided not to go into any more detail, and he made her an unsecured loan.

J.D. and the Cotton Gin

Electric power came to Lenox sometime in the 1930s with Georgia Power Co. Shortly after electricity was available, one of J.D.'s customers, Mr. Griner, learned that cotton gins had now gone modern and were powered by electricity.

Mr. Griner approached J.D. about borrowing the money to purchase and install an electric cotton gin in Lenox. J.D. was very impressed by the idea since there was a lot of cotton being grown in and around the Lenox area and

Mr. Griner would have the first of the new, modern electric gins, so he readily approved the loan.

After the gin was up and running for the cotton harvesting season, Mr. Griner invited J.D. to come over and have a demonstration of the fancy, high tech gin.

As Mr. Griner was demonstrating the operation, something clogged up the mechanism and the gin came to a halt. Mr. Griner unplugged the gin and since J.D. was standing next to where the clog was, he asked if J.D. would mind just pulling the door up, reaching inside and pulling the clog out. He said, as soon as you have it cleared, let me know and I'll plug it back up.

J.D. did as he was instructed and grabbed the clog. He told Mr. Griner he was pulling it out, but Mr. Griner, who was hard of hearing, thought J.D. had said, "plug it back in."

Fortunately for J.D., he had removed his arm out far enough that it was intact when the gin started back up again, but one of the gin's knives clipped off the end of his nose.

From that time on, when people met J.D. for the first time, many would ask what happened to his nose. J.D. would reply," It got cut off sticking it into somebody else's business."

Grandaddy Henderson

My grandfather Henderson was a Civil War Veteran who settled in Adel after the war.

During the war, he was trained as a demolition expert. In Adel, he set up a blacksmith shop on the North East corner of the city block where the Adel Wesleyan Church is today. A boarding house was located on the North West corner of the same block and was noted for the excellent Sunday meals they provided.

The blacksmithing profession required a lot of coal to heat up metals enough they could be formed in any way the smithy desired. At that time, coal could not be obtained in Adel so he was forced to cut large hardwood timber, split it into smaller pieces and season it for many months before it was usable. As a result of all that labor, his wood stack had great value to him.

One day he opened up the blacksmith shop and immediately noticed some of his hard-earned fire logs were missing. He became very angry and was determined to find out who had stolen his wood. He immediately decided how he could catch the thief. He bored a small hole in the end of a wooden log and filled it full of black gunpowder. In order to conceal the hole, he took some mud off the ground and covered over the hole. Then he placed the log in a place where he would know where it was, but a thief would not.

The next Sunday morning as the Church sang Amazing Grace just before they ended their service, a loud explosion was heard coming from the boarding house next door. Everyone rushed over to see what had happened at the boarding house. What they discovered was the wood fired stove had been blown off its base and there were chicken and dumplings all over the ceiling.

From that day forward, grand-dad Henderson had no more fire logs stolen from his blacksmith shop.

Robinson Uncle Stories

One of my uncles on my father's side was not a very pleasant person. He seemed to be sour on the whole world. One day he was hanging out at Mr. Ralph Lindsey's Hardware Store with the usual "lazy bench crowd", catching up on all the latest Lenox gossip.

One of the men remarked that they were having a very spirit filled revival at the Lenox Baptist Church. Another man looked at Uncle A and said, "Why don't you come tonight and join us?"

Sour as he was, Uncle A replied that he would not be going to that church because it was full of hypocrites. One of the other men turned to face Uncle A and said with a serious expression on his face, "Well, there's always room for one more."

Uncle A never joined the lazy bench crowd again.

Uncle B

I always looked forward to Uncle B coming by the bank and visiting with me because he was so entertaining. He had a very dry sense of humor, but he could be hilarious. He was very active on the political scene and would work tirelessly for the candidate of his choice.

Uncle B eventually got smitten with politics and decided to run for the office of Mayor of Lenox. When the votes were counted, he had received a mere 8 votes. It was a humiliating defeat.

The next day, he drove up to Mr. Harry Shaw's Supermarket where another lazy bench crowd met each day. When he parked his car, all eyes were on him as he opened the car door. He had a big pistol strapped to his hip, and one brave soul asked, "Mr. B, why do you have that big pistol strapped on today?" Uncle B replied, "Anybody with no more friends than me better be packing a big pistol."

Uncle B and the Cabbage

Uncle B was driving past a farmer friend's house one day and noticed the farmer had a beautiful field of cabbages. Uncle B loved cabbage and he stopped at the farmer's home to pay a visit and buy a couple of cabbage heads.

The farmer invited B in for a visit, but B told him he wanted to buy two heads of cabbage. The farmer said, "I'm not sure a man your age is allowed to buy cabbages or not." Uncle B responded, "Why not?"

The farmer said he had planted a new variety of cabbage that had the same effect on men over 70 as Viagra. Not missing a beat, Uncle B replied," Well, in that case, I don't want two cabbages, how much do you want for the whole damn field?"

Uncle B, The Election Supervisor

Uncle B became elections supervisor for the City of Lenox and he was a stickler for going right by the book. He would allow no exceptions.

An important Presidential election was in process and everything was going very smoothly when a car drove up to the door of the voting precinct. The door to the building was glass which made it possible for anyone in the car to be visible from inside the precinct. Inside the car was an elderly woman who was being helped by her son. The woman was not able to get out of the car easily and walk inside.

The son went inside and requested a ballot for his mother. Election workers knowing how strict Uncle B was about following the rules, told the man they could not allow that since it was against the rules. Ballots were not allowed to leave the building.

The son was determined to let his mother vote, so he asked to be allowed to speak with the supervisor. The worker explained the situation to Uncle B. She pointed out that the woman was within view seated in her son's car just outside the door.

Uncle B told the worker to bring the son into his office. He explained that even though he wanted the elderly woman to be allowed to vote, the rules required a voter to be present inside the voting site.

The son pleaded with Uncle B who finally softened up a little and he asked, "By the way, do you know how your mother was planning to vote?" The son replied, "Oh yes, she always votes a straight republican ballot."

Upon hearing this, Uncle B instructed the election worker to give that poor woman a damn ballot!" UU

Uncle Glynn

My mother and her only brother, Glynn Welch, grew up in Milledgeville, Georgia. For some reason, the State of Georgia had established a Military School in Milledgeville by the name of GMC, Georgia Military College. The school also enrolled boys for high school, tuition free.

Uncle Glynn attended GMC in high school, but he was not interested in academics. He wanted a job so he could start making his own way in life. The Greyhound Bus Station in Milledgeville, was located between GMC and the Welch home. One day as he was on his way to school, he saw a sign in the window of the bus station which read, "Help Wanted".

Glynn decided to inquire about the job, so he went inside and was told the bus company was hiring a driver for the trip from Milledgeville to Atlanta and back each day. The pay sounded good to Glynn, so he applied for the job. The problem was Glynn had never been to Atlanta before. He knew where the highway was, but he certainly had no idea of what Atlanta was like or where the bus station there was.

In a few days, he stopped back by the station and was told he had been hired for the job. Glynn was excited, but he knew he couldn't tell his parents because they would not allow him to quit school. Glynn decided that what his parents didn't know would not do any harm.

His first day began as he put on his GMC military uniform each morning, grabbed a stack of school books and pretended to be going off to school. In reality, he would walk to the bus station, change into a Greyhound

Bus Driver's uniform and make the run from Milledgeville to Atlanta and back. That first trip was quit a trip. He drove through town and onto the Atlanta Highway, not knowing anything else. When he arrived in Atlanta, he drove around town in circles looking for the

Greyhound Bus Station. Eventually, he stopped for a street light where a policeman was standing next to the curb. Glynn asked him for directions to the bus station and finally delivered his passengers. The whole bus shouted with relief when he pulled into the station.

When he returned home, he would change back to his school uniform and go home. His new job remained a secret, until school grades were sent home and his parents discovered he had missed school every day. That was the end of his Greyhound career.

Grandaddy Welch and the Empty Hearse

My grandfather on my mother's side, for whom I was named, was a mortician in Milledgeville, Ga.

Late one night, my grandfather received a call from the State Mental hospital there saying a patient had died and he needed to send a hearse to pick up the body and prepare it for burial.

Grandfather called the mortuary and instructed the employee on duty to go pick up the body.

The driver reached the hospital and backed the hearse up to the doorway where employees would bring out the body and load it into the hearse.

As he was waiting, a pretty young nurse caught his attention and the driver paid no attention to what was going on around him.

The body was placed in back of the hearse while the driver was still making eyes with the nurse.

While the driver was not looking, a drunk staggered around the corner of the building and laid down in back of the hearse and fell sound asleep.

The driver finally decided to close the door to the hearse and drive back to the mortuary.

On his way back into town, the driver stopped at a red light. While he was waiting for the light to change, the drunk woke up and pulled out a cigarette but he needed a light. He rose up in back and said to the driver," Hey buddy, can you give me a light?"

A few minutes later my granddad received a call from the Milledgeville Police. The officer said he needed to go down to the stop light and retrieve the hearse. When he arrived, the driver's door was open, the engine was still running. The driver never returned to work at the mortuary again.

The Adel Drive-In Theatre

During the 1950s and 1960s, drive in theatres were at their prime. The theatre in Adel was named the Rio, but the huge sign on back of the screen actually read, "R10".

One summer, the theatre was in the middle of playing a "double header" when a beat-up old pickup truck came to a screeching halt at the ticket booth. The driver told the clerk he was not buying a ticket because he would only be inside a short time. He said he had been told his wife was in the theatre with another man, and he had come to "take care of things." The clerk knew he was serious because he could see the sawed-off shotgun laying across his lap.

As the husband sped into the theatre, the ticket agent got on the theatre's public address system and announced; if there is anybody in the theatre with someone else's wife, you better leave because the husband is on his way in with a sawed-off shotgun.

For just a second, there was total silence. Then it was reported that 5 automobiles cranked up simultaneously and made a mad dash for the exit, leaving the husband bewildered in a cloud of dust.

The Fishing Pole

An older customer was in my office one day and she reported the following story. She said one Sunday afternoon her family was visiting with her on her porch and they observed a pickup truck turn off the road and drive down, a dirt path on her property which led to the river.

The lady told one of her sons to go run the trespassers off her farm. The son did as she instructed, and found the truck parked next to the river.

The son approached the truck and knocked on the window. A moment later, an unclothed man emerged from the truck. The son asked what he was doing there.

The man replied that he and his girlfriend were just there to do “a little fishing.”

The son replied, I can see your fishing pole, but take it and your girlfriend and go fishing somewhere else.

The Ambulance

Back in the 1950s and 1960s, ambulances and EMTs didn't exist. Mortuary hearses did double duty. If you were dead, they carried your body to the cemetery, but if you were sick, they carried you to the hospital.

A patient in the Adel hospital was near death, and his physician called a local mortuary to come immediately to pick up the patient. He instructed the driver that if the patient had any chance to live, he would have to get him to the hospital in Albany as quickly as possible.

The driver replied, "Yes sir, the road is mine!" The hearse drove away from Adel in a cloud of dust on U. S.

Highway 41 headed North to Tifton, then West to the hospital in Albany.

The driver was so focused on getting to Albany as quickly as possible, he didn't notice that the rear door of the hearse was not completely closed.

As he drove up the highway overpass between Adel and Sparks, the rear door opened and the patient fell out as the patient rolled down the hill strapped to the stretcher.

Some bystanders saw what had happened and rescued the patient and removed him off the road.

The Sparks policeman was informed and he immediately called the policeman in Lenox. The Lenox Policeman was able to stop the hearse and inform the driver he had left his patient back at the overpass.

The driver immediately turned back, picked up his patient and finally delivered him to the Albany hospital.

The remarkable thing is that the patient survived!

The Doctor and the Plumber

A local doctor and plumber were close friends since grade school.

One day, the plumber's wife became very ill during the night and was running a high fever. The plumber was worried if she was not seen before morning, something awful might happened. It was late, but he decided to call his friend, the doctor and ask if he would come over and attend to his wife.

The doctor was home trying to relax after a long, hard day when the telephone next to his bed rang. He listened to his friend describe his wife's symptoms and decided her condition to wait until morning. He told the plumber that his wife would be fine, just give her two aspirin and call him in the morning.

The plumber was infuriated at the doctor's seeming lack of concern, but he didn't make a scene about it.

Some months later, the doctor was at home one night when his toiled became clogged up and overflowed. Water was everywhere. The doctor immediately thought of his friend, the plumber and called him. He told the plumber all the details about the problem and how he had not been able to stop the flow of water.

The plumber instantly recognized the opportunity to get back at the doctor. His reply was that the problem didn't sound like an emergency and to flush two aspirin and call him in the morning.

The China Berry Tree

When my wife and I were building our home, an older customer of mine dropped by one day to see how the construction was going. It was at that point he related the following story.

He was around the age of 11 or twelve when he and his siblings were hoeing cotton on his father's farm, that is known as Staunton, sometime after the turn of the twentieth century. He said they had heard of airplanes, but had never seen one.

As they were hoeing, they heard a strange sound in the sky overhead. They looked up and there was the first airplane they had ever seen. The plane's engine was sputtering and they saw the plane descending a few miles north of where they were working.

They immediately dropped their hoes and started walking toward the location the airplane had gone down. He said people all over the area had observed the same strange sight and they were all on their way to see this strange machine. Most people were walking and some were riding mules. The site the plane had landed on was in the field just across from where our new home was under construction. The farm was 490 acres in size and required many farm hands to keep it tended. He said there were a lot of farm houses on the farm, just across the road from our home.

The plane's engine had malfunctioned, but the pilot was able to land it safely on the field. One of the older farm hands was taking a noontime break as he slept comfortably under the shade of an old China Berry tree.

The strange noise of the plane's engine sputtering on and off only a few yards behind him frightened him so much, he had a heart attack and died immediately.

Uncle Mose

Growing up in the 1950s, I loved tagging along with my dad. He loved people and he never seemed to meet a stranger. He was just as comfortable talking with a college professor as he was with a farm hand.

On one occasion I hopped in the car with him and as we drove up U. S. 41 highway North, he said he wanted me to meet Uncle Mose. Uncle Mose was over 100 years old and had been born into slavery.

A few miles up the road from Lenox, he turned onto a dirt road that was lined with many farm tenant houses. There was a white-haired, older-looking African-American sitting on the porch of his tenant house.

We stopped and daddy introduced me to Uncle Mose and we sat down on his porch. Daddy and Uncle Mose talked about a wide range of subjects ranging from the weather, how the crops were doing to politics.

I played around the yard a bit, then I heard my daddy ask Uncle Mose a question I didn't fully understand at the time. He asked, "Uncle Mose, tell me, how old does a man have to get before he stops thinking about the ladies?"

Uncle Mose rubbed his whiskered chin as if he were in deep thought, then he replied, "I don't know, Mr. Roby, you better axe somebody older than me!"

The Mail Train

Back when a regular size letter could be mailed with a 2-cent stamp and before the labor unions took over the postal service, our mail system was a very different beast. Mail was delivered efficiently and on time. Today, after decades of bureaucratic "streamlining", the U.S. Mail system bears no resemblance to the service we took for granted in the 1950s.

I used to be fascinated with how the system worked back then. If you wanted to get a letter to Tifton or even Macon, all you had to do was purchase a 2-cent stamp, have your letter in the mail box downtown by 10:00 am.

Then your letter would be delivered the same day, in most cases for most nearby towns, it would be in the recipient's mail box before noon, the same day.

The system went something like this: The local postmaster would gather all the outgoing mail and get it sorted by destination. Then he put it all in a heavy, canvas bag that he would take over to the railroad track nearby. There was a pole near the tracks where he would hang the mail bag and wait for the next train.

Almost every train had a mail car. When the train went by, never slowing down, a clerk in the mail car would lower a metal rod that would catch the mail bag the local postmaster had placed on the pole.

Inside the mail car, you could see several postal workers sorting mail to be dropped at the next stop. When the train passed through Tifton, for instance, all the mail from Lenox would be tossed out inside a canvas bag which a Tifton postal clerk was waiting. Then it would be placed in the recipients box the same morning it was mailed from all the towns along the way north.

Aunt Mary Crawford

My aunt Marie Crawford inherited a nice farm in West Berrien County. She was a very loving person who took great pride in her family's background. She grew up in the period of the great depression, which taught her the value of work in addition to the practice of frugality.

One day her husband, Lawrence, was away from home when she decided to make the short ride from her home in Cook County to her Berrien County farm just to see that everything was in order.

During those years, there was a large sawmill company in Cook County that had a reputation, deserved or not, of crossing over land lines and cutting timber of adjoining owners without their permission.

When she arrived at her Berrien County farm, she observed crews of that company cutting timber on the farm adjacent to hers. She saw that they were getting very close to her timber and decided to take precautionary measures.

Marie drove home, retrieved her husband's double barreled shotgun and returned to the site where the timber was being harvested.

The timber crew had indeed crossed over the line and were cutting her timber.

The crew was busy with their job and never noticed as she slowly walked up behind them and pulled back the hammers of the shotgun. There was no need for any conversation.

The crew threw down their equipment and fled the scene.

Moral to this story: Don't mess with a country girl!

The Policeman and the Farmer's Wife

A local farmer suspected his wife was cheating on him, so he devised to plan to determine one way or the other. He suspected the Lenox Policeman was the other man.

The time period was before interstate 75 was constructed and U.S. 41 was the main North, South highway. The Lenox Policeman had a booth, somewhat larger than a phone booth, next to the highway and the Lenox stoplight. He would seek shelter there during adverse weather conditions while he could observe the heavy traffic on the adjacent highway.

One day the farmer drove up and parked next to the police booth with a fishing boat and trailer in tow. He told the policeman he was going on a three-day fishing trip down to Orange Lake, Florida. After they talked a few minutes, the farmer walked across the street to a service station and purchased a Coca Cola. He started his truck and drove away Southbound.

Unknown to the policeman, the farmer drove to Sparks and turned around. When he returned parked outside his home. Evidently the policeman must have heard him coming in and he ran out the back door, unclothed.

The Lenox Mayor was called to go out and fetch the police car.

My Uncle Lawrence Crawford

My uncle Lawrence once related the following incident he was party to in his early teens.

Uncle Lawrence grew up in North Carolina in a small town where there was a policeman who was overzealous in stopping teen drivers for even the slightest infringement.

A group of teens, including Lawrence, decided to teach the policeman a lesson. His favorite post was parking under the shade of an old oak tree in town. Sometimes, he became drowsy and would drift off to sleep.

The teens discovered him asleep one night and their plan was set into motion. They had a long, strong logging chain and tied one end to the police car's rear axle and the other end around the oak tree. They were very quiet and the policeman never heard what they were doing. Next, they loaded into a farm truck and drove by the policeman as fast as the truck would go, blowing the horn.

The Policeman was startled from his nap and started the engine. He was excited at the thought of making another arrest. He put the gear into the drive position and hit the accelerator to the floor. The car immediately lurched forward as the chain became taught and snatched the rear axle from under the car. The policeman was left still grasping the wheel, not understanding exactly what just happened.

A Dog Story

Growing up, our family always had pets around. We had one particular dog that stands out in my memory. Naturally, every pet must have a name and ours was no exception.

Santa delivered an adorable, red, Chinese Chow puppy one Christmas morning. We considered a multitude of names and finally settled on the name "Ching."

The name just seemed very appropriate for a Chinese dog. It didn't take long for us to become very attached to Ching and he was very spoiled. Ching was very loving and protective of his family, but Ching had an alter ego. Ching had a thick coat of fur that made him appear much larger than he really was.

As he grew up, Ching became a bully in the neighborhood. He beat up all the other dogs of the neighborhood. One time, he somehow gained entrance to a neighbor's chicken yard and actually killed one of her chickens.

We took Ching to Doctor Bozeman in Adel when he developed an awful looking rash, and the diagnosis was the dreaded, mange. The Vet said there was only one way the mange could be treated effectively, and that would be to shave all his fur off and treat the affected areas with some kind of purple medication.

When we brought Ching home, he looked like a completely different dog. He was physically small in appearance and weird looking with the purple medication all over his bare skin.

It wasn't long before all the other dogs in the neighborhood that Ching had bullied before, suddenly realized they had nothing to fear. It became "pay back" time for Ching, and we finally had to bring him inside until his fur grew out again.

Saddam & Sheila

Sometime ago, an unwanted couple decided to try and move into our backyard.

Unwanted? YES! They were skunks. They left their "perfume" all around our house. This was about the time Saddam Hussein was terrorizing the world from Iraq. It was reported he had even used poison gas on his own people, just to test the effectiveness of the poison.

I was determined to rid our yard of these two invaders, so I got out my hunting rifle. I had not used it in a long time so I started practice shooting for a shot to the end of our long yard. After a few practices, my shooting skill was restored.

I planned a simple ambush for the varmints. I placed the hunting rifle next to the patio door. In that position, I could sit at our breakfast table and scan the yard. Then when the stinky varmints appeared, all I had to do was take my rifle, open the door and eliminate the invaders.

Not long after, I got my first chance when the couple appeared about half way up toward the house. I was excited to finally have a chance to give these unwanted pests their just rewards.

My first shot missed one of them by a millimeter, but enough to make him enraged. He turned around and started backing up toward me.

I immediately knew what was coming when he raised his tail and jacked up his hind legs. I closed the door and told Margaret to shut off all the air conditioners, we were under a gas attack.

Needless to say, that was a costly bad shot, but we survived and I was more determined than ever to take the pair out.

The next encounter was more successful as my aim was true and the two invaders met their fate.

The next question was how to deal with the remains. I decided the best method would be cremation. It was the fall of the year and we had loads of pine cones on the ground, so I tossed a generous amount of pine cones over the bodies and ended their reign of terror.

So that is the story of Saddam and Sheila and the gas attack near Lenox.

The "Generous" Tip

When our family was growing up, we all looked forward to spending a week at St. Augustine, Florida. We had a favorite condo we booked every year and we became very familiar with all the establishments in the area.

We would take one day each year driving to Orlando where the kids had a good time and then driving back to the condo late that night. We also enjoyed going to the docks where the shrimp boats came back with fresh caught shrimp and crabs that Margaret would cook for a sumptuous meal.

Some days the children played at the beach all day and we didn't want to cook or go out to eat. One such day, I ordered a couple of large pizzas from a nearby restaurant to be delivered to where we were staying.

I remembered approximately how much they cost from the previous year, so had the money ready on the table for when it would be delivered.

Soon, the doorbell rang and I gave Warren, Jr. the money I had ready for the delivery boy and told him to go to the door and pay for the purchase. I estimated that I had included a generous tip, so Warren, Jr. took the pizzas and handed the money to the delivery boy. He told him to keep the change! He said the delivery boy looked at him with a disappointed look, but he didn't know why.

When he brought the pizzas to the table, I glanced at the bill and to my surprise, the "generous" tip amounted to only 3-cents.

We returned the following summer and during our stay, we ordered another pizza from the same restaurant. This time, the clerk made a point to tell me exactly how much the bill was and the usual tip amount. They had remembered us from the previous year!

All Hat and No Cattle

There was a small farmer in the Lenox area who loved tending to his black angus cattle. He was the kind of person who got totally immersed in whatever endeavor he chose to pursue.

His small herd was his pride and joy. He started attending meetings of various cattlemen's associations and gained a lot of knowledge about raising cattle. He would attend such meetings and if you didn't know, you would get the impression he was a very large cattleman.

On one occasion, he was elected President of the State Cattleman's Association. He was an excellent President and performed his duties well.

At one of his meetings, someone suggested since they had a lot of new members it seemed appropriate for everyone to stand and introduce themselves.

One by one, each member rose and gave a brief account of who he was, where his farm was located, and how many cattle he managed.

One member would report he owned 750 acres and managed 500 cows. Another would report he owned 2,000 acres and managed 1,200 cows.

It finally became time for the Lenox farmer to introduce himself and he didn't quite know what to say. Just then, his wife blurted out, "Go ahead and tell them, you have 5 cows, you have 5 cows!"

The Consummate Salesman

One of our local "characters" was working as a convenience store clerk when he noticed an expensive car had parked out front, but the occupant stayed inside the car.

Since it was after dark, he could not actually see the occupant, but he became very suspicious. As long as there were shoppers in the store, the mysterious person remained inside the fancy automobile.

Finally, there were no other customers in the store, and an impeccably dressed older woman emerged from the car and quickly enter the store. She immediately approached the clerk and stated she needed some advice on selecting a condom.

Being the consummate salesman, he never showed any hint of emotion. He instructed the lady to follow him to the area where the item she sought was located. One by one, he gave her information about the pros and cons of each item.

The lady finally asked for his recommendation. The salesman turned and looked the lady up and down.

Finally, he replied, “Judging from what I can see, I would recommend this particular item. It’s called The Rough Rider.”

A PhD from the School of Hard Knocks

Just after World War II, a Lenox Veteran returned home safely and one of his few possessions was an Army Surplus truck. He was eager to go to work, but he had a limited education and jobs in Lenox were almost non-existent. What he lacked in formal education though, he more than made up with a keen business acumen.

It is said his dad gave him a closed up old gas station in Lenox on highway 41. He used that old army truck to drive down to a gasoline terminal in Florida, buy a load of gas at wholesale prices, drive back to Lenox and sell the gas 3 cents cheaper than the competition.

With sheer guts and hard work, the young man built a large chain of gasoline/convenience stations he named, "Dixie Oil Company."

Later he became a member of an association in his profession. The meetings would often ask new members to introduce themselves and give some background information.

Some would proudly share their biographies making a point to brag about attending Harvard or Yale or some other high-class school.

Our Lenox man was prepared. He had gone to Athens to check on one of his stations, and while he was there, he parked at the University of Georgia Administration Building and walked through.

When his turn came, he stood up proudly and announced how many stations he owned and that he had gone through the University of Georgia.

A Lenox Legend – Otis Lindsey

Otis grew up in a hardworking family that had survived the Great Depression through the sweat of their brow. Otis was a happy-go-lucky, devil-may-care young man when World War II reared its devastating head on the world in the 1940s.

After entering the Army Air Corps, Otis was assigned to Robins Army Air Base in Warner Robins, Georgia for training as a fighter pilot. Otis was a natural born pilot who would spit the devil in the face. He had no fear.

After Otis completed pilot training in Warner Robins, he wanted everyone in his little hometown to know he had become a pilot. It is reported Otis took off from Warner Robins and flew his plane South, following the railroad tracks to his hometown of Lenox to let everybody there know he was now a pilot. Otis flew at top speed over the railroad tracks that divide Lenox making a statement, that "Otis was here", breaking every storefront window in town.

After the war, Otis was a farmer, a rural mail carrier and a crop duster. When Otis wanted a fresh fish dinner, he would fly his crop-dusting plane to Bank's Lake, just outside Lakeland, Georgia, and land on the highway. Purchase fresh caught fish from the fish house and fly back home to have his wife prepare a fresh fish dinner.

The Policeman and The Radar Gun

Officer Melvin Dove was another Lenox character who could keep you laughing until your sides burst.

The City of Lenox purchased one of the first traffic control radar guns, and Officer Dove was sent to a class for instruction about the use of the new device.

One afternoon, Officer Dove stopped by the bank where Judge Lott and I were having a conversation just outside the entrance.

Judge Lott seemed a bit skeptical about the accuracy of these new contraptions and he asked Melvin to demonstrate it to him.

As instructed, Melvin held up the device and aimed it at an automobile passing through town, obviously at a slow speed; however, the radar gun indicated the car was going in excess of 50 mph.

Still skeptical, Judge Lott instructed Melvin to aim the gun at the house across the street. Melvin did as instructed and the radar gun indicated the house was moving at a speed of 45 MPH, confirming the Judge's skepticism.

The Farmer Who Won the Sweepstakes

A local farmer had a brother who was the local rural mail carrier. He noticed his brother often entered The Publisher's Clearing House Sweepstakes Contest. The winner of the contest would be surprised at home when the company would ring the doorbell and announce they were the winner of a huge prize amount.

The mail carrier decided to have some fun at his brother's expense. He had someone call the farmer who would not be recognized, and announce he had won the grand prize and they would be delivering the check the following day.

The caller also instructed him that it was suggested he and his wife dress up as they would be filming the presentation of the check.

The next day came and the farmer and his wife were dressed as instructed and waiting on the front porch of their home for the film crew to drive up for the presentation. Just then, the mail carrier drove by on his normal route and wave to them with a huge grin as he passed by.

The Businessman, and the Joke

A well-known businessman from the County had a medical condition that required an immediate bathroom response.

One day he was cruising down the interstate highway with several of his buddies, just hanging out. Suddenly, nature called while they were far from any restroom, so the driver stopped on the highway apron and the plan was to provide their buddy some privacy from passing motorist, by opening the front and rear passenger doors while he did his business in between, out of sight.

The businessman was known for his outlandish pranks on his buddies, so now they all knew it was payback time. As he was occupied squatting with his pants down, his friends closed both doors and drove away, leaving him exposed to all the oncoming traffic.

He vowed he would get even with them if it was the last thing he ever did.

The Gambler

A group of local men had a gambling game in a nearby town every Saturday night. Citizens near the location complained regularly to the Sheriff, because they didn't want that kind of behavior going on next to them and there was a constant noise coming from the location that kept them up at night. One of the members was a man who had told his wife that he was going to those games every week, when in fact, he was using that as an excuse to have a night with his lover.

The Sheriff warned the group that if they continued, he would have no choice but to arrest them.

The group didn't stop and eventually the Sheriff was forced to raid the games and make arrests.

The news of the arrests spread quickly throughout the county. The following Monday morning, the cheating husband was seated in front of the Sheriff's desk. It was widely known that a list of names arrested at the games would be published in the following week's local newspaper.

The cheating man told the Sheriff that although he was not present when the arrests happened, his name had better damned well be on the list when the newspaper was published.

www.ingramcontent.com/pod-product-compliance
Lightning Source LLC
LaVergne TN
LVHW010611110826
845149LV00003B/859
* 9 7 9 8 9 9 5 6 4 2 3 6 7 *